Instead of Maps

Instead of Maps

Kim Bridgford

David Robert Books

Published by David Robert Books
P.O. Box 541106
Cincinnati, OH 45254-1106

Typeset in Aldine by WordTech Communications LLC,
Cincinnati, OH

ISBN: 1933456000
LCCN: 2005926430

Poetry Editor: Kevin Walzer
Business Editor: Lori Jareo

Visit us on the web at www.davidrobertbooks.com

Author photo: Pete Duval
Cover image: Jo Yarrington

Acknowledgments

Abbeywood: "Elizabeth Bishop," "Sylvia Plath"
Acumen: "The Moment"
Candelabrum: "Lies"
The Chariton Review: "In Passing," "Madness"
The Chattahoochee Review: "Loss"
The Christian Science Monitor: "Emily Dickinson"
The Classical Outlook: "Jocasta," "Oedipus," "The Sphinx"
Connecticut Poetry Review: "Lies"
The Formalist: "Robert Frost"
The Iowa Review: "Echo," "Offerings"
The Listening Eye: "There Was a Boy Who Killed Himself"
New Zoo Poetry Review: "Satan"
Pivot: "Eden's Gift," "Satan Redux," "Time," "The Wishes"
Poet Lore: "One Hundredth Birthday"
Poetry Nottingham International: "In Love with the Past"
Rattapallax: "History," "Tag Sale"
Seam: "In a Stranger's House," "Satan"
South Carolina Review: "Along the Edges," "Anorexic Sonnet," "It's
    Something Near"
Valparaiso Poetry Review: "Remembrance"
Wascana Review: "Instead of Maps"
Willow Review: "Her Sister's Hands"

"Emily Dickinson" and "Anne Sexton" appeared in *Undone*,
published by David Robert Books, 2003.

"Robert Frost" will appear in *Visiting Frost: Poems Inspired by the Life
and Work of Robert Frost*, University of Iowa Press, 2005.

"Along the Edges," "Eden's Gift," "Instead of Maps," "It's Something Near," "Lies," "Loss," and "Time" will appear in *Eden's Gift*, forthcoming from Aralia Press.

My writing colleagues at Fairfield, both past and present, have been essential to my development as a poet, and I would like to acknowledge them here: Janet Krauss, Nicholas Rinaldi, Tony Sanders, and Michael C. White. In addition, I am grateful for the community at the West Chester Poetry Conference, particularly Michael Peich and Dana Gioia.

Many of the poems here would not have been written without the financial support of the Connecticut Commission on the Arts, Fairfield University, and the National Endowment for the Arts. I appreciate the artistic commitment of all of these institutions.

Thanks to Lori Jareo and Kevin Walzer, my editors, and to Jo Yarrington, cover artist, colleague, and friend.

And, finally, I am grateful to my parents, Ken and Carole Bridgford, for their love and support.

For Pete and for Nick, always,

and in memory of Agha Shahid Ali,

Jamie Hulley,

and Donald Justice

Contents

I.

Emily Dickinson

I think about the days she sewed her poems
With threads of ink that held the sounds between
The words. She put her heart down in her rhymes
And understood that somewhere in the skin
There is an answer for each line, a chorus
That she traced within herself. Why pause
Right there? a student asks as if to stress
The point. The answer is in earthly laws
Of conversation, how to frame them so
The texture of the momentary speech
Lasts. Think of your memory as a ragged row
Of utterances that you would like to reach
For when you wished. Impossible. She chose
To try: with words—then dashes—between those.

Frank Lloyd Wright

Every great architect is—necessarily—a great poet.
He must be a great original interpreter of his time, his day, his age.
— Frank Lloyd Wright

He was a man who made himself a myth,
For there are those who see life differently,
Whose taste for grandeur cuts another cloth,
Who pierce the center of conformity.

He was a man like that. Who doesn't want
To live inside his dream? To feel the hearth
And floor and walls as architecture meant
To be a clear extension from the earth.

The nymphs that lived to sanctify the wood
Were something, then, that Wright had understood.
It's natural to have a spirit living there
As if the tree's interior were a chair.
The sound of water, the shadow of a tree:
All part of myth and myth's morality.

Robert Frost

You seemed to know the most about the dark,
But softened it, so we would listen, still
As leaves before they show they're vulnerable
To wind. You seemed to know the grief of work,
And also joy, depending on the weather
And how the critics saw your poems. You seemed
To know how tragedy could happen, aimed
At no one, but simple as a signature.

You seemed to be the voice that spoke the poems:
Genial, meandering, New England to the core.
And yet you never were; you played the part.
The mask you wore enabled the extremes:
The truth that fingers ice and whispers fire.
It was the neighbor's voice that made it art.

Wallace Stevens

He sold insurance in Connecticut,
But blackbirds and a jar in Tennessee
Made him forget the whole insurance racket.
Imagination was reality:

And suddenly the world was Sunday morning,
Or snow inside a snow man's mind. He taught
That what we know can shift, inside a turning,
Like gradual variations of the light.

His marriage wasn't happy, but he worked.
At work he wasn't happy; he came home.
The mind set out to find a new address.
Illusion took his hand, and they embarked
To hear the blue guitar and eat ice cream,
Where *be* was *seem*'s finale out of loss.

William Carlos Williams

The thing itself was all he cared about.
It was as if he pared the world away,
And left the core of what he meant to say.
Similes and metaphors were out.

Instead the glimpse: the moment gleaming there,
The beauty found in the pedestrian—
The chickens, the red wheelbarrow, and the rain—
When life and death both glistened in the air.

A pediatrician, Williams understood
The poet's carpe diem attitude.
A poet, Williams tried to "make it new"
The way a doctor has been trained to do.
As both, he knew each baby and each poem
Depended on the hands that brought them home.

Marianne Moore

It's hard to get to know you, Marianne.
You shield yourself with animals and fish,
With facts, with words that dangle with a hyphen,
The stanzas antiquarian and brash.

And yet I love your eccentricities:
You're like an aunt who knows just how to please,
But keeps her secrets locked up in a drawer.
Who says confession's what a poem is for?

"Imaginary gardens with real toads"—
Your poems are real but not reality,
Like lions built in stone to speak of creeds
Live ones can't know. Your quirks are legendary—

The Brooklyn Dodgers, your lovely tricorn hat.
Is it fair to ask for any more than that?

Elizabeth Bishop

Maps. Florida. Brazil. A waiting room.
As much as you can conjure up a place
From words that smell like oranges or home
(The *National Geographic* on your knees

Unwinding your new self into a cry),
It is the explanation of your loss—
Your father, mother, lover, family,
Umbrellas, keys, the timbre of a voice—

That makes me stop, the moments that we leave:
The tired travelers sitting on a bus
Trading life stories until with a great heave
They are startled by the candor of a moose,

The moment that grinds to a halt and is gone
Or delivered (right it!) like a fish undone.

Anne Sexton

In all the pictures you are smiling, sexy,
Beautiful. You seduced the audience,
Trembling as you offered up your demons.

Striptease. Soultease. Naked in your poetry,
You lay there, quiet, sucking on your death;
Then something called you back: the blood and music
Of your art. The wandering poet of the sick,
You stood at podiums and howled the truth.

No audience on the last day. Alone,
Wrapped in your mother's coat, the music on,
You said good-bye to everything you knew.
You who gave yourself to love, to sun,
To writing, you who were brilliant and insane,
Made all the words line up and mourn for you.

Sylvia Plath

I think I know what you were thinking then:
You lay in death's lap, waiting to be mothered.
Love wouldn't let you go, pulled you back in.

In hospital, you discovered love had won,
Each needle frightening like the pulse of God.
I think I know what you were thinking then.

Later, the babies helped, and your husband;
Travel, bees, work. Yet sometimes nothing could.
Love wouldn't let you go, pulled you back in.

But you were up at five with poems that were written
In blood; and still they came, harboring your dread.
I think I know what you were thinking then.

The night was hardest: the moths, helpless, drawn
To the light; you listened to what darkness said.
Love wouldn't let you go, pulled you back in.

One day they came and scraped your stone
While you tapped out the Morse code of the dead.
I think I know what you were thinking then:
Love wouldn't let you go, pulled you back in.

The Artist

For Jamie Hulley (1981-2002)

You wanted to create, to be like God,
To shape a vision out of swirling cloud,
To raise the Adams up, and lovely Eves,
To write the sunlight falling on the leaves,
The place where possibility can stir,
The tremulous unfolding of the air:
The narratives that come from paradise.

And when you died, we saw through your own eyes:
The paradox of the unreached-for fruit,
The vision of what was and what was not
Unraveling, like knowledge from the trees.
In loss is also metamorphosis.
We saw in a reversal from our grief
The Eden you had left us leaf by leaf.

II.

What If

What if, we say, we'd left the moment there—
The way we might a sweater on a chair—
And with one extra morning cup, the car
That sent our lives careening was not far
But somewhere up the road? What if the choice
Could just be redirected by a voice,
A bird's insistent warning that could change
The one event that we would rearrange?

We play our what-ifs over every day
As if in doing so we'd find a way
To make our moments easier to live.
Why don't we think of the alternative?
Convinced that we could, somehow, lift our curse,
We never think we could have make it worse.

Remembrance

The past is nothing but lost remembrance
We sift through hands that want to set things right.
We want to give our lives significance;

And perhaps we can—the blazing utterance
We see now with the gift of second sight.
Yet the past is nothing but lost remembrance,

Not facts. Don't count on a continuance
Of scenes: unholy hands, words replayed at night.
We want to give our lives significance;

We want to make sense of the circumstance.
But the memories shift, and we can't get them quite.
The past is nothing but lost remembrance.

These lips and hands are our inheritance;
They are the only gift we hold outright.
We want to give our lives significance.

The present is the saving brilliance
In small bits of extinguishable light.
The past is nothing but lost remembrance;
We want to give our lives significance.

It's Something Near

There it is again. It's something near—
An insect, or a fork scraping on bone.
I feel it like the underside of fear,

Small, but brimming with particular
Detail: like glyphs translating out of stone.
There it is again. It's something near.

Madness starts with this—a singular
Moment that recurs in isolation.
I feel it like the underside of fear.

Hidden. Rasping. Terrible. And there.
Sometimes I'm left with just this one sensation.
There it is again. It's something near

And intimate: a finger on a star,
The breathless escalation of a passion.
I feel it like the underside of fear,

The pulse of life and death, a cockleburr
That does not let go. In my skeleton
There it is again. It's something near;
I feel it like the underside of fear.

Madness

Madness doesn't always kill;
It can lie dormant in the deepest bones,
And, like a piece of sky, remember things
You thought were gone: impossible
That smoke against the blue. like private stones
Sent scattered; impossible the twilight.
You wonder why your hand begins to shake
As you pour tea, like medicine, in lamp-light.

When love can't heal you fast enough,
You walk down roads as if a something will,
But, while spilt water over rocks can cure
A moment's wrong, it isn't proof
That hearts know how to be more versatile.
You pause to see a couple kiss
In lighted windows framing their embrace:
They kiss the tips of metamorphosis.

Madness gravitates to tableau
The way the water laps its lilting tongue
On rock. On Sundays you sit full of need
As startling as vertigo,
As sure as swans that amble in their throne
Of watery silence. A child cries
Out for nurse-maid to look up, and she
Does not, with an insolence you recognize.

You sift through notions of the past
To see if they can leave a graceful nothing
The way sand does. But scenes conform to shapes

That travel loosely through the glass,
Not like time's funnel, rushing with a gathering
Weight to muteness. The past has voice
That speaks in hyperbolic tones, or else,
Like gnats, in bursts of thick inconsequence.

Madness is a sorrow deep
As bells, sturdy as their grip, a moment's tongue
Giving brittleness to air. Sometimes
You can't believe the way you keep
Your skeleton from pealing out a wrong
Your skin keeps quiet and in place.
A disturbance to the slightest touch of skin,
Like foreign fingertips along your face,

Is like the love-shudder awry
If butterflies could speak their folded trembling
Through the lips of loss. Then the day
You learn such madness is a lie,
The suffering that you have in common
With everyone. At this impasse
You look back on a bewilderment of snow
And ahead to your forgetfulness.

Insomniacs

The world is full of people who can't sleep.
Yet every sleepless person feels alone.
Each passing thought is like a burning ship,

While dreamers swim in coolness, far and deep,
Leaving in their wake what might have been.
The world is full of people who can't sleep.

At 3 a.m., they rattle every friendship;
They whisper jagged kisses to the phone.
Each passing thought is like a burning ship

Upon which stands the one without a rope,
Who knows, no matter what, he's going down.
The world is full of people who can't sleep.

Yet insomniacs don't want to hear the grope
Of lovers staying up to come undone.
Each passing thought is like burning ship.

Finally through death's hallway they will creep,
And lie in answer to their sleepless question.
The world is full of people who can't sleep.
Each passing thought is like a burning ship.

Anorexic Sonnet

I am in love with pins, with my own bones
Revealed in near transparency, with idea.
In fact, I'd love to live where thought disowns
Whatever holds it fast to earth. Medusa
Understood: the body's nothing, just
A statue form. To crack it open, reveal
The spirit trapped forever in the dust
And watch it, in its arrogance of smile,
Fly off: That's all I've wanted. To undo
The architecture of my days and rise,
Up, up the rungs of angels and of Plato—
The drifting forms of pure philosophies—
To where the stars make room. I want to die
But not to die. The trouble is the body.

Her Sister's Hands

Her sister never walked, but pulled her length
Across the floor, in an elaborate
Shimmy of the boards. Everyone took her strength

For granted, and that her hands were immaculate,
More beautiful than the poses of a star
Flinging her boa back, saying, "It's late.

I must be getting home." She went as far
As the bedroom and back, and each day rose in her hands.
She flexed her fingers, beautiful, as pure

As statue hands, and she lowered her shrunken ends
Down, those legs like little tentacles
And caught herself, worked herself through the bends

And footboards of the house. Her miracles
Were daily, and they were part of her, just like
Her name—Helen—the sunlight on her nails,

The house beneath her body. You'd think to wake
To this would be too much. Of course it was.
Yet she loved the taste and burnish of a cake,

Marbles in her fingers, and the careful squeeze
Of her body through a chair. Where'd Helen go?
And then she'd twist the length of her surprise

Out for laughter. When the state came through
To check on children meant to go to school,
There she was, and that was it. She knew

It would be different, when they came to pull
Her from her family. Then she was gone.
They put her in a mental hospital.

And why they thought this place they put her in
Could be a better mother, she couldn't say.
She listened to the voices trapped like sin

Until they spoke to her as well. The day
Her family came to see her, she knew them
Only as shapes that came and went away.

She crawled until the floorboards grew so dim
She stopped. That's when the snake became a lamb.

Poetry

There are the days I cannot stop my dreams.
I think I'm capable of anything:
Those days I see the brightness as it gleams
On leaves and petals as they're opening;

But then the other days I see them halted—
Held captive in the muck with stick and stone.
Discouraged, I'm cut off from the exalted,
A prisoner of mortality and bone.

Yet it's from this give and take, this sun and mud,
This spectrum ranging from the stars to blood,
That something happens that I recognize:
The marriage of my failure with a stream.
Hope, barefoot in the splash of writing's dream,
Picks up the words like angels in disguise.

Let's Hear It for Hyperbole

To pull the moon out from behind its swag
Of cloud and hang it like a prop, is, well,
Corny, and yet who wouldn't do it, beg
That poetic push would come to shove, the swell

Of overstatement in a fit of love?
The body offering its hidden jewels
(And not-so-hidden-ones) makes you believe
That only language circumventing rules

Could speak to what's beyond the ordinary—
What's greater than, what's deeper than—to love
The soul that speaks through eyes, lips red as a cherry.
Then, daily conversation's not enough,

And only words that trumpet with pizzazz
Will show us how life wasn't and now is.

Along the Edges

Some days it's easier to dwell on things
That rim the edges of her life: the blue
Flowers of her cup in thin enamelings
She drinks from, or the slat of sun cast through
The blinds. The veins in fork-lines at her wrist
Can make her pause, or the smallest mole
That checks the beauty of her mouth. What's lost
Is speculation on her life: the whole
Versus the parts. She'd rather see the petals
Drop and note the quiet of their fall
Than see their death; she'd rather hear the riddles
Of her father's madness sent like hail
Than understand the silence of his gaze,
The shuttered eyelids closing on his days.

The Wishes

I threw a penny in a well.
I wished for the impossible.
I wished for grief to hide its tail.

I threw a penny in a stream.
I chose a clear and steady aim.
I parted ripples of my dream.

I threw a penny in a river.
I felt that I could live forever.
Somewhere within I felt a shiver.

I threw a penny in a sea.
I knew that I had wished a lie
Eaten by the fishes swimming by.

I threw a penny in the air.
I knew a wish was just despair
Hanging in the sunlight there.

There Was a Boy Who Killed Himself

There was a boy who killed himself because
He felt the pause

Within the beats of time, because the hymn
Of death would climb

Like chords, until the music broke upon
Itself. Within

Himself he tapped a cave where he found all
The beautiful

Dying: old people, babies, the friends he knew
Who died in snow,

The world grown quiet along their windshield.
No one would hold

Him again—not mother, not girlfriend—
Nor would the sound

Of rain make him glad. The dark lullaby
Of his good-bye

Would plume out of the back of cars in smoke.
There was an ache

In his soul the night he climbed into his death.
There was a moth;

There was a sense of fate; there was a thing
That broke in song;

There was a darkness tangling the rakes
And the heartaches

Of the living who would think of him and say,
There was a boy,

And speak the fables of his loss, the lamb
Who gave *I am*

To death, and with each crossing of the sun
There would be one

More day without him, what he had not known
In that last dawn.

One Hundredth Birthday

Your birthdays now are lit with irony,
And years build up like tombstones on the cake.
You use one candle for simplicity.

Anticipation mixes with an ache
That makes you wonder how you got this far,
And when. At thirty, things became a blur,
And then the weary nonsense of the rest.
One hundredth birthday bash! It's a mistake,
You say, and they count out for you, alike,
With rapid fingers all your days. No test:
You can't believe you are three numbers strong.

You've become a span of time where people go
To reevaluate where man went wrong.
Time's diplomat, you smile, and then you blow.

Tag Sale

You look for treasures in the heaps of junk:
Ceramic dinnerware, stuffed animals,
Posters of forgotten movie idols,
Books with pages missing, and you think—
Someone once cared about these things. Now strangers
Tear apart the yard, while the family sits
Behind card tables selling dollar hats
That Grandma wore to church. You see the dangers
In thinking that the past is over because
Somebody's dead. A cup's enamelled rose
Reveals that you have grown more sentimental
About the lost, rag tag, and ornamental.
Yet afterwards, the things that you take home
Seem weightless, like the Sundays lost in them.

The Moment

The Buddhists are right; the moment's gone,
So that's why when a lover from the past
Surprises us somewhere, our heart is thin
With breath, our body must try to resist

The person it once was, the scent it knows
Like spring, or pain—an unaccustomed thirst—
And feel the present slipping off like clothes.
Is that what frightens us? The way we burst

Open like a fruit at merest chance,
The way our physicality will dance?
When we are different now, we say. We say
It again. Better not to know the way
Our body is not our body, but the skin
Of someone else we lost and found again.

History

What is the past but a deserted road?
Someone once lived there, reading on the porch
With the light on. Someone once turned and said,
"I'll be in soon." The moment felt like church,
Palpable with God.
                    One day the house
Disappeared to rooms where paper dropped
Away from walls, where mice ate up the lease
And memories drifted out, like dust that's swept
Into the wind.
                    There will be time to walk
That road, and feel days lifted like the leaves
Traveling nowhere. Sometimes the ghosts will squeak
Like the hinges of memory pried away from grooves:
This is what you were, and what you'll be
Forever: nostalgic for your own decay.

In a Stranger's House

The past is like a bed in a stranger's house.
Naked, you wrap yourself inside the sheets;
Yet you're not sure you'll ever like this place.

Whose breath is that you feel? Whose wan nightdress
Slips out when you slip in? One of the fates'?
The past is like a bed in a stranger's house,

While down the hall sleep loneliness and loss.
You're back in childhood, feeling for the lights;
Yet you're not sure you'll ever like this place.

One lover whispers, *Cruel*; another's voice
Begs to be let in on windy nights.
The past is like a bed in a stranger's house.

Day will not come. Night brings the hoot-owl's peace,
And soft, like old umbrellas, hang the bats.
Yet you're not sure you'll ever like this place.

One day you wander in. You'll stay unless
The house burns down: then marvel at the rats.
The past is like a bed in a stranger's house;
Yet you're not sure you'll ever like this place.

In Love with the Past

I don't live in the moment, never have,
Don't know how to. The past rattles me
With its whispers, like kisses on my sleeve,
Hot through the material. It makes me cry
With its slow tunes like a serenade of earth
Before the world was made. Then it makes love.
A good lover, its fingers are the heft and hearth
Of what I know. When it says it has to leave,
I beg for time; already it's not there,
Half-listening to silence, to a grave
Where mourners kiss the curdles of their fear,
And, trembling, sift through shadows more alive
Than life. Come back, I say through shifting speech,
And wait for one barbed memory to catch.

Lies

I find the truth has nothing more to say.
Lie to me. Tell me that beneath this face
You see the one you kissed when a good-bye
Took hours. Tell me that there is not a place
You'd rather be than in this hospital,
Where I hold the missing music of my breast
And die. Then tell me the impossible:
How I will live. Now everything is lost,
So sing to me of beauty and of love.
I know you love me; never did I doubt.
I need the trick of lies to help me grieve.
Tell me in the end good will win out.
Tell me that when the worms find out my home
You'll force their blindness from my catacomb.

Time

Unable to articulate the past,
You fall to grieving time: it's in us all,
This mournfulness for things that cannot last,
The what-ifs calling, each lost interval
Remembered as an open place of green,
Where light arrays the moment with its awe
And trees hold out their arms to intervene
Before the future comes. Yet there's no law
That says that time would glitter in its trace;
Instead the dark could harbor its deceit,
And your regrets no chance at breathing-space.
Worse still, your longing simply could repeat
Forever: watching life in pantomime
Unfolding with the blemishes of time.

What the Others Say

We want to know what all the others say
When we are suffering from embarrassment,
And in so doing give our lives a way

To give a shape to pain and to the day.
When we do well, we want not just the moment;
We want to know what all the others say.

The champagne pours. There's a glitter of confetti.
It's the way we celebrate accomplishment—
And in so doing give our lives a way

To feel that we are someone, and a way
To endure those nights when all the nightmares haunt.
We want to know what all the others say.

What happens to our selves as visions play?
They wince and falter, knowing disappointment,
And in so doing give our lives a way

To move their smallness through another day.
We walk in fallen graveyards without comment.
We want to know what all the others say
And in so doing give our lives away.

Instead of Maps

You wonder if you'll ever know the way
You should have walked, or if such things as maps
Have anything to offer life. A stray
Residue of leaf, caught on the careless steps
Of the wind, says more; or, better yet, the fog
Some mornings, when place is where you once were,
The air like dreams. With hands outstretched, you beg,
Then simply move. There's nothing else. A star,
Some nights, is all you have, with grass gone cold
And distance blurred with loss. When the body dies,
There's nothing more to touch, the moment stilled
To something like the aftermath of lies.
If that's the lesson, there's no way to go
That stops the drifting surfaces of snow.

How

How sometimes what should be said isn't said.
How words elude the touch of hands in bed.
How a friend we haven't seen we hear is dead.
How we are left with nothingness instead.

How sometimes just the sky fills us with need;
How birds and snow know quiet as they fly;
How we just feel this, gathering inside.

How we say we'll keep in touch, but mostly lie.

How sometimes when time passes we will see
The way our parents, and their parents too,
Unravel in our skin and memory.
How children echo us as we pass through.

How feeling makes us think that others know
How much they've meant to us. And it's not so.

Loss

In cancer wards, in leaves, our love, and skin,
Loss lies beneath our hope and happiness.
It's always there: the buried skeleton
That is remembered even with a kiss.

Loss lies beneath our hope and happiness.
It's known at birth: the savage traveling
That is remembered even with a kiss,
Like the scent of someone who will not live long.

It's known at birth: the savage traveling
Over the world, the paths weary with dust
Like the scent of someone who will not live long,
And we all travel them because we must.

Over the world, the paths weary with dust
Lead to beds, hospitals, home and nowhere,
And we all travel them because we must.
We've never learned to breathe another air.

It's always there: the buried skeleton
In cancer wards, in leaves, our love, and skin.

Eden's Gift

The darkness held within a flower's bloom,
Undone in curling fragrance by the sill,
Sickens the heart. But why? In every womb
There's loss to drink, in every birth the chill
Of merciless abandonment. To us,
The tender terror on the crucifix—
All that blood wonder—is miraculous,
But, daily, wildness gorges on the mix
Of life and death. Some deep forgetfulness
Allows us time to love, and laugh, and hold
This gift of Eden far from happiness;
And yet sometimes a resurrected cold
Will seize us by a flower in a vase,
Relentless as the skull beneath the face.

III.

Echo

Echo: The Adolescent

He'll never look at me, I just know it.
Yet I could stand here, like the merest leaf
Until my feelings murmur in their grief:
Love you, love you, love you. I don't regret
The offerings I leave in watered shrine:
He touches them, the things that once were mine.

Don't give me pity but the surest way
To make him kiss me, see himself in me.
They say, *Narcissus sees his own reflection,*
And then, *Narcissus will only break your heart.*
My heart, I say. If he finds satisfaction
In the rippling of my skin, I'll play that part.
Someday he'll see me too. In my body's glass
He'll see the woman there beneath the surface.

Echo: The Woman

He didn't see me, nor has ever seen
The self I offered; now I want to leave.
I can't, I can't, I can't. The reflection in
My mirror stops me, makes me want to grieve
For who I was and what I'll never have.
Who will want me now? Who will know to love
The girl who sang her love song on her grave?

He liked the first encounter. Love was thin,
But love is love. That was my theory then.
Now my dreams are different: not a man
Whose love is practice. Instead a bookish one,
A man who knows the way to love a woman,
Beyond the body, but through the body's skin.
To him I'll say: *Again, again, again.*

Oedipus

I discovered that a door is just a door.
To sleep with Mother is the fantasy
Of every little boy, and yet I'll say
That once you've done it, let the inner ear
Tell you what you have always known, it's like
Something in you knows a joke and winks
At the same time as your frightened conscience blinks.
I saw and didn't see; a cataract
Made all my worries possible to bear.
Because I think my body must have known.
Because I loved her, and lay with her in bed.
Because her skin and mine were like the air
I breathed. Because, as king, I had no stain.
Because some blindness is confused with good.

Jocasta

It wasn't wrong because we didn't know,
But we weren't children, except that you were mine.
A myth is truth that's fashioned by the throne.
You have the power to circumvent the law.

Because our love cannot accommodate
A way of seeing that causes so much pain;
Because, no doubt, we'd do it all again,
For power, and love, and what we'll accept as fate.

Because, my darling, evil's just a way
To sort the world for those with nothing else.
Give me your eyes, and I will see with them.
I'll offer you pure sexual fantasy.
The common people will see us and our curse
As more than their morality can claim.

The Sphinx

Grow up. Go on. You think that others live
In worlds where what they want is what they get?
You have much more than most, and all the rot
Of sin is something covered with your love.
Because that's what adults must learn to do.
It's making something good from what's been lost
That makes you something better than a beast.
Rule wisely. Open up your eyes, and grow.
It's boys that throw a tantrum on the bed.
It's boys that curse the living and the dead.
It's boys that sleep with Mama and confess.
It's boys that curse their fathers and their loss.
It's men that learn that sex, and myth, and war,
Are what those boys have all been waiting for.

IV.

Satan

I was in love with all of them: as if
The true democracy of death outlined
Their predilections, so the shadowed ground
Was like an exercise in bas-relief,
Showing, through art, the way they all had sinned.
I was there, always, to greet them coming off
The boat. They recognized me by my cough
And by the way I took them by the hand
And led them into gloom, where they'd know love
Of fire, and worms, blind tunnels home to slaves.
No reason to look back, when up above
Hypocrisy would blur what made them mine.
Welcome, I said. They simply saw themselves
Inside. They once were kings but sang like swine.

Satan Redux

I'm struck by the inefficiency of good—
Just how unlike a factory it is—
All done by hand, and no apparent use
Except to the poor, and they might as well be dead.
I run the reasons over in my mind,
And find that evil's path is easier,
More lucrative, and sets the waiting fire
That licks the sins that hollow humankind.
Yet still, old women buttoned tight in wool
And old men praying to a cut-out God
From Sunday school have hope I can't assail.
Nuns, gull-like in their habits, fly with food
To men and women skeletal from AIDS.
They lift their necks to life and what it feeds.

Offerings

Mary

What does God-sex feel like? Is it the thrill
Of looking at the sun, or the slow tremor
That shakes the body like a miracle?
Is it the arrow piercing through the armor?

Or is it nothing but the feeling that
Something new is just about to happen:
A flower unfurling, the shaping of a thought,
The idea of an apple made to ripen?

The impossible for you was like a cup
You drank from, and you, in turn, believed
That when you suffered you were lifted up
And when you trusted you were also loved.
Like any mother, you were filled with hope,
The world now just the husk where he arrived.

Joseph

You loved her, and it didn't matter what
The others said. You knew what she'd been through,
And if the story strained, you said, "Tell it
Again." And she did until she saw the world in you.
That kind of love is called a miracle.
At night you curled into each other's hips,
But sometimes you would think how she would call
The sunrise God, the dazzle made of shapes
That otherwise would merely hold a space.
So what. You'd be the shadow to that sun;
You'd be the father to her quickened child.
If on the changing sky, she saw His face,
You thought that she'd forget. "Our child is the one."
"Our," she said. "Our." And you were reconciled.

Jesus

It's the only family that I ever knew,
And I loved them. Yet poets always know
They're born to live another kind of life:
The hyperbolic dailiness of grief.
I looked: I saw the homeless and the sick.
I listened to the ordinary music
Of prayer, of wind like breath along the sand,
And in them felt both oracle and end.

And when He spoke to me, I called him Father.
He was my Muse, this iridescent Other,
His knowledge rubbed like oil against my skin.
He opened up my spirit, like the weather,
And when I spoke, we made the poems together.
He said I'd live forever, till I'd listen.

God

I am so perfect, sitting in the skies.
To prove that I would gladly sacrifice
Through blood, who am immortal and alive,
I'll offer up my son. That way I'll grieve
The way that humans understand: to lose
What matters most, the thing they'd never choose.
I'll choose it; I am perfect, being God.
My son is the embodiment of good.
I will not hold him yet. He'll have a woman
On the earth to raise him into what is human,
And later he will meet me on a cloud
And tell me what it was to be allowed
To walk upon the earth, with bitterness,
And know the thorns that I could only guess.

V.

In Passing

I.

If he tries hard enough, he can know love.
When did he first feel this way? He supposes
When he held his breath, so that he'd have
His mother sleeping in her nightgown, roses
Breathing with her for a hour, and then she'd wake
And make her coffee, pull the cord of blinds
Until the world snapped open. She would take
His hand and point it at the dazzled fronds
Of day, then up to the planes. He left a smudge.
When he went off to school, he watched her go:
Her mouth, her hands, the insides of her knees
And tried to catch the ravel of an edge.
She's dead now. He tucked her in the earth, with snow.
If he tries hard enough, he can know peace.

II.

If he tries hard enough, he can know peace.
He thinks about the ways he's found to be
In a circle of contentment, of the days
He remembers for their ceaseless harmony.
Not many. One day he was on a knoll,
And he looked up from his reading; the text
Held on a moment to his eyes, and all
The natural world was like a palimpsest.
For a while before the words went down
He read the world as if the shadows there
Were translations of the contemplative.
And when he blinked, the fragile words were gone.
He thinks of that, when he sees things on the air.
It's just a state of mind. He's learned to grieve.

III.

It's just a state of mind. He's learned to grieve.
How easy it is, like breathing, like the whir
Of the heart. When he was sitting on a grave,
One summer, he thought he heard the bones, a blur
Of clacking white beneath the ground, like voices
Gossiping about what they barely remember,
More like the worms in their slow distant faces,
And mild, burrowed in the crevices of timber.
This is what is sad to him, the names
From long ago known only by their script.
He'd like to know the details he should miss—
A fingering of hair, the secret shames—
But he knows nothing eloquent is kept.
He's learned the sudden curdle of a promise.

IV.

He's learned the sudden curdle of a promise,
And then there's nothing but what might have been,
Which is the story of lost paradise.
Sin is nothing but the continual refrain
Of love, betrayal, and loss. *Oh, how could*
You do this to me?: then the punishment
That makes the childish moment turn to dread.
Nothing brings back innocence. What's spent
Is spent. *I don't love you. I'm going away.*
How could you have been with someone else?
Explain to me. I just don't understand.
Then she is gone, and the texture of the day
Hurts him. Later, he can navigate the loss;
He can step off, into a new land.

V.

He can step off, into a new land,
A strange and melancholy wilderness.
He's lost, until he sees he's not defined
By the mythical tale of one lost trespass.
Not only fear can constitute a life
But also joy. He learns to laugh again
And lingers on a moment's bas-relief:
The filmy silence lifted from the dawn
In veils that almost lose what's following them.
It's a gentler way of being on the earth:
Learning how to savor each surprise
By stopping in the held note of the hymn.
Yet sometimes moments come to him by stealth
With his old life appearing by degrees.

VI.

With his old life appearing by degrees,
How can he live? These are the mocking voices
That wake him up at 3 a.m., his eyes
Dried with bits of wakefulness, his choices
Made of mud. He is surprised at how
This feeling can pass, just as a simple cup
Of coffee can change the way the day will go.
Then he will look back on what kept him up,
And it is shocking, like a revelation
About a friend. This buried secret changes
The moment, the startled cough in *I have sinned,*
But otherwise relieves the conversation.
There is truth for once. A sameness impinges,
Ghostly, like letters in a stranger's hand.

VII.

Ghostly, like letters in a stranger's hand,
These tricks of eye. Each curlicue and slant
Reflects essential meaning. It's the end,
After all, that matters. So he's spent
Days on things that mattered most, and still
The daylight funnels off too soon. Felt time
Oozes with panic. Birds eat their fill
From his blueberry bush, and the bruised gleam
Of the berries makes him pause. He cannot stop
Their theft, unless he picks the berries hard
And nearly green. If he could only seize
Something with that intensity, each drop
Whole and new. It's true, as in a word,
The smallest change can trigger a surprise.

VIII.

The smallest change can trigger a surprise:
A flick of movement from a frog, a moth
Giving up the dark for startled frieze
Of light, the rain, the momentary wreath
Of a kiss, made different by its wayward push.
What lies beneath the mapwork of his skin?
With shift in knowledge, there's the after-hush,
And the world is new by traveling within.
The hinge that brings the body to its joy
Is perhaps the greatest blink of time,
The come-cry held between what's almost there,
And then release. The moment is the key,
With gold the texture like a fingered rim.
Why not some happiness? Why not some air?

IX.

Why not some happiness? Why not some air?
At the carnival, he finds he is amazed
At how the children revel in their fear,
Each moment sticky as the moment prized
By appetite. And when he bites the cotton candy
It is sweet; and when he rides the ferris wheel
It is higher than he dreamed, the windy
Night like little currents. His body's thrill
In silver seat beside the Tilt-a-Whirl
Bears him so that his mind is quiet and calm.
There, for a time, he is no longer afraid.
Later he will drive to a meadow and lie still
And watch the lights evaporate like film.
Lying in the dark he turns his head.

X.

Lying in the dark, he turns his head,
And he wants to walk through the silky corn
Of his childhood days, feel the simple nod
Of stalks as he imagines the day he was born:
How he was pulled from the bloody lap of his mother
For the world, then tucked and fed and scrubbed and held
So he could live and have these thoughts, no other
But himself. Circumstance made him the child
To whom the others brought their deepest faith.
The awe of this is like some mythic force
That brings to humans an immortal test
Through love or skill or losing life to death.
Every day he thinks the fight is worse
Because he sees the shadows of his past.

XI.

Because he sees the shadows of his past,
And they say nothing about what drives it all,
He is afraid. He's told that it's the least
By which he will be judged, the trivial
Lined up for an inspection of his life.
And he winces from it, winces at what he could
Have done, how his tremendous grief
At this means nothing but *what if* and *should.*
He would like to be remembered, not
For being able to get along, but for
Changing those he loved by being there.
He thinks that this is what life's all about,
A subtle change that marks the atmosphere,
Like flames that tease with color, then aren't there.

XII.

Like flames that tease with color, then aren't there,
The angels that he pictures lolling in space
And humming, not in choirs, but in the clear
Abstracted way that comes with happiness.
He supposes that his view of the after-life
Is just this life, yet more so: like a picture
Brought in focus, so that even brief
Expressions have a lasting signature.
Yet he is troubled when the sins he knows
Seem freshest, and his sense of shame is high;
The simple hallelujah starts to fade
To vapor trails, and then to nothingness,
In short, the doubt within hyperbole.
When he closes his eyes, he sees some stars instead.

XIII.

When he closes his eyes he sees some stars instead,
The days he calls his life. How rich, how few,
How paltry, and how loved. It is what he wanted,
He knows, and what he couldn't bear. Each crow
Of death is a harbinger of life, the greed
That knocks the day upon its knees to take
The air; yet he holds firm the parchment creed
That ruffles feathers and relieves the ache.
When he thinks of death, he thinks of when
He made a leap of faith, a dive that meant,
In all its vertigo, to save what's lost.
Now, in the stomach drop of in between
He jumps and curls into a somersault,
Going beyond the universe at last.

XIV.

Going beyond the universe at last,
He feels the quiet gathering of hands,
Prayer maybe, or the bells that feast
In tinntinnabulations of their sounds.
He falls. Birds gather, scratching out their stake,
Then whir, like hope, into a multitude
Of wings. He thinks of his mother, and the ache
Of sunlight on her breast. Whatever's said
About the trouble of all human life,
There's a beauty in the commonplace,
The shadows on a face, a brushing sleeve,
What's made in passing, and what's made in grief:
The paradox of what he wants to trace.
If he tries hard enough, he can know love.

XV.

If he tries hard enough, he can know love;
If he tries hard enough, he can know peace.
It's just a state of mind. He's learned to grieve.
He's learned the sudden curdle of a promise;
He can step off, into a new land,
With his old life appearing by degrees,
Ghostly, like letters in a stranger's hand.
The smallest change can trigger a surprise.
Why not some happiness? Why not some air?
Lying in the dark, he turns his head
Because he sees the shadows of his past,
Like flames that tease with color, then aren't there.
When he closes his eyes, he sees some stars instead,
Going beyond the universe at last.

About the Author

Kim Bridgford received an M.F.A. from the Iowa Writers' Workshop and a Ph.D. from the University of Illinois. She lives with her husband, the writer Pete Duval, and their son, Nick, in Connecticut, where she is a professor of English at Fairfield University and editor of *Dogwood*. Her poetry has appeared in *The North American Review*, *The Christian Science Monitor*, and *The Georgia Review*, her fiction in *Redbook*, *The Massachusetts Review*, and *Witness*. She has received fellowships from the NEA and the Connecticut Commission on the Arts, and in 1994 was named Connecticut Professor of the Year by the Carnegie Foundation for the Advancement of Teaching. Her book *Undone* was published by David Robert Books in 2003 and nominated for the Pulitzer Prize, and her chapbook *Eden's Gift* is forthcoming from Aralia Press.

About the Artist

Jo Yarrington is a professor in the Department of Visual and Performing Arts, Fairfield University, Fairfield, CT. Her sculptures, photographs, and installation pieces have been shown in exhibitions at Artists Space and The Cathedral Church of St. John the Divine in New York, Rotunda Gallery in Brooklyn, the Aldrich Museum of Contemporary Art in Connecticut, the DeCordova Museum and Sculpture Park in Massachusetts, I Space Gallery in Chicago, Glasgow School of Art and Glasgow University in Scotland, Galleria Sala Uno in Rome and Christus Church in Cologne, Germany. She is a recipient of fellowships from the Pollock Krasner Foundation, Pennsylvania Council on the Arts, the Brandywine Institute, the Leighten Artists Colony (Canada) and the MacDowell Colony.

Printed in the United States
40116LVS00007B/369